YOUR FAMILY TREE

Beginning Genealogy

by Jim Ollhoff

Why Genealogy?

Have you ever wondered why your nose is shaped the way it is? Ever wondered why you have the color hair you have? Ever wondered why you are tall or short? Many of your characteristics have been passed down to you from your parents, grandparents, and earlier ancestors.

Genealogy is the study of your ancestors. You had 2 parents, 4 grandparents, 8 great-grandparents, and 16 great-great-grandparents. If any one of them didn't exist, you wouldn't be here, either. In genealogy, we learn about the people who helped make us what we are.

When did your family first move to this country? Where did they come from? How did they make a living? Did your great-grandfather fight in World War I or II? Building a family tree can be a giant puzzle, where you get clues and discover your ancestors and information about them. To be a successful genealogist, you need to be a detective, finding obscure information and putting together pieces of the puzzle.

Below: If any one of your many ancestors didn't exist, you wouldn't exist, either.

Photographs and documents can help us learn about long-lost relatives.

What Does Your Last Name Mean?

Below: Singer John Denver took his surname from his favorite Colorado city: Denver. His birth name was Henry John Deutschendorf.

Last names are also called surnames. Through most of human history, people didn't have surnames. People lived in small villages and on farms, and everyone knew "Fred" or "Marianne." But in Europe, between 1000 and 1500 AD, villages started getting bigger. Travel and trade became more important. Suddenly, a village might find itself with six Freds and four Mariannes. So, people started using additional names so they could tell each other apart. These additions eventually became surnames. In Europe, there were four main ways that people got their surnames.

The most common kind of surname was based on parents' names. So, Fred might become "Fred, son of John." This eventually became Fred Johnson. In Ireland, the capital O meant "son of." So "Finian, Son of Malley" eventually became Finian O'Malley.

Another kind of surname was based on geography. For example, a person from the city of Muenster would be known as Fred of Muenster, which eventually became Fred Muenster. Marianne, who lived near a brook, might become known as Marianne Brook.

Above: In Ireland, the capital O meant "son of." So, "Finian, Son of Malley" eventually became Finian O'Malley.

 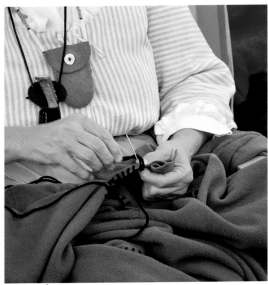

Above: A person's job sometimes provided a surname.

Another way of getting a surname was through a person's job. Fred the tailor became known as Fred Tailor. In Germany, the "er" at the end of a name often means "one who." So, "Fred the one who makes shoes" eventually became known as Fred Schumacher.

Another way of getting a surname was through physical traits. "Fred who is strong" became known as Fred Strong. "Marianne who has black hair" became known as Marianne Black. Probably less than 10 percent of surnames come from this method.

In other countries, such as China, surnames were used much earlier than in Europe. The earliest Chinese surnames were only for royalty and very rich people. As time went on, people took the name of the state where they lived, or their tribe, or the name of an ancestor.

Above: The Chinese family name Chen (often spelled as "Chan" in English), comes from a region in China's Henan Province.

Surnames may provide some clues to your ancestry, but you can't stop there! Some family names seem to have no explanation. There are a few reasons why a surname is not a perfect way to get family history clues. One problem is that before surnames became important, people sometimes switched their surnames. Fred the Shoe Maker might go to work for John the Wheat Farmer. So, Fred would change his name from Fred Schumacher to Fred Wheatley.

Above: Some family surnames seem to have no explanation. An ancestor may have changed his surname when he changed professions. Or he may have changed the spelling to Americanize his name.

Another problem for genealogists is that people who came to the United States often Americanized their name. Fred Muenster might change his name to Fred Munster. Marianne Koenig might change her name to Marianne King (Koenig is a German word for King).

A third problem, and a very common problem for genealogists, is spelling. Today, it's very important to spell names correctly. But the idea of "one correct spelling" only came about in the late 1800s and the beginning of the1900s. Names were often spelled like they sounded. People wrote them many different ways. For example, the name Joeckel might be spelled Jackel, Yackel, or Yokel.

State _New York_

County _New York_

Township or other division of county _Manhattan Boro_

Incorporated place _New York City_

Ward of city _6th Assembly_ Block No. _C_

Unincorporated place

Institution

Enumerated by m

Above: 1930 census sheets show how the spelling of surnames varied. Highlighted in yellow, these New York families spelled their names Joeckel, Jackel, Yackel, and Yokel. They may have all been related.

Genealogy Golden Rules

Below: Some jobs that were common in the past are no longer familiar to us. It is important to record as many details as possible.

When you start working on your family tree, there are some golden rules you should follow. These rules will save you a lot of time and energy as you learn about your family history. Think of yourself as a detective who has to solve the mystery of your missing family members.

Golden Rule #1: Record the Source

Where did you hear that story about Grandma Bertha? Where did you see that Great-Grandpa Hector was a squirrel inspector? Write it down. After you've heard 10 stories about Grandma Bertha and Great-Grandpa Hector, you'll probably forget where you got them. Write down who told you the information. Write down that you saw in the 1910 city directory that Hector was a squirrel inspector. Record all your sources. This will save you a lot of time and energy later.

Above: Record as much family history as possible. Be sure to include who gave you the information. If you later have additional questions, you'll know who to ask.

Golden Rule #2: Keep it Organized

If you stay interested in genealogy, you could become the family historian. Family members will start giving you old photographs and items of interest. Make sure you write down who's in each photo. Make sure you attach a note to that old, tattered wedding dress so you'll remember who was married in it. Keep all your family memorabilia in a special place, where it won't get damaged or lost.

Golden Rule #3: Don't Believe Everything

How do you know that Grandpa Farnsworth's father was named Archibald? Did you hear it from Cousin Frank, or do you have a birth certificate? Always make a distinction between sources. A good primary source is usually something that was recorded while the person it concerns was alive— for example a birth or wedding certificate. Family lore is a story that is passed down through family members. While family lore can be very valuable, it's often wrong, or incomplete. Don't trust family lore as the sole authority, unless it's backed up by a primary source. In fact, many times primary sources are wrong, too. Don't trust any single source with 100 percent certainty.

Golden Rule #4: Write It All Down

Write down as much as you can. Not just where your sources came from, but all the details, too. The smallest detail about Grandpa Farnsworth might help you later. Think of every detail as a piece of a puzzle. Your job is to put all those pieces together.

Golden Rule #5: Don't Get Frustrated

If genealogy were easy, then everyone would do it. You'll run up against a lot of brick walls and dead ends. Keep going! The information you need is probably out there somewhere. You just have to find it. Genealogical research takes a lot of patience.

Above: Write down as much information as you can. Small details may help you later.

Family Trees

One of the first steps you should take is creating your family tree. A family tree shows parents and children as far as you can go backwards in time. Sometimes this is called a pedigree chart.

Illustration 1 (page 17) is an example of Fred O'Malley's direct ancestor family tree. This kind of family tree starts with one person, then lists their parents, their parents' parents, and so on. It doesn't include any brothers or sisters, aunts or uncles, or cousins. Family trees are usually designed in the same way. Since this is Fred O'Malley's pedigree chart, he puts his name on the left side of the page. To the right are his parents. Fathers always go on the top of the chart. Fred's father is Thomas O'Malley.

Fred's mother is Marianne Yackel. Mothers always are written on the bottom of the chart. Always use the maiden name of the mother—the name with which they were born.

Fred's grandfather is Farnsworth O'Malley. Farnsworth is the father of Fred's father. Farnsworth would be considered Fred's paternal grandfather, since *paternal* means "on his father's side." Fred's paternal grandmother, or his father's mother, is Marie Buntrup. Remember, this is Marie's maiden name, not her married name.

Fred's grandfather on his mother's side is Gunther Yackel. This is Fred's maternal grandfather—*maternal* means "on his mother's side." Fred's maternal grandmother is Linda Barnswallow.

Direct Ancestor Family Tree

Farnsworth O'Malley
Your Father's Father
(Your Paternal Grandfather)

Thomas O'Malley
Your Father's Name

Marie Buntrup
Your Father's Mother
(Your Paternal Grandmother)

Fred O'Malley
Your Name

Gunther Yackel
Your Mother's Father
(Your Maternal Grandfather)

Marianne Yackel
Your Mother's
Maiden Name

Linda Barnswallow
Your Mother's Mother
(Your Maternal Grandmother)

Illustration 1

17

As you draw your own family tree, you might not yet know all the information. For example, you might not know the name of your paternal grandfather. If so, just write "unknown" in the blank space. Or, for example, if you know his last name was Johnson but don't know his first name, then write "Unknown Johnson." If the first name is Vlad, but you don't know the last name, then write "Vlad Unknown."

At this point, include only your direct ancestors. Write down your biological parents. Don't worry if they are divorced or remarried—include only the parents who gave you birth.

Don't worry yet about brothers, sisters, cousins, uncles, and aunts. The broad family trees that include these relatives are called *collateral family trees*. Right now, just work on your direct ancestor family tree.

Facing Page: You may photocopy page 19 and fill it in to create your own direct ancestor family tree.

Below: A direct ancestor family tree includes yourself, your parents, and your grandparents.

Direct Ancestor Family Tree

Your Father's Father
(Your Paternal Grandfather)

Your Father's Name

Your Father's Mother
(Your Paternal Grandmother)

Your Name

Your Mother's Father
(Your Maternal Grandfather)

Your Mother's
Maiden Name

Your Mother's Mother
(Your Maternal Grandmother)

Myths in Genealogy

Above: You can research your family tree at Ancestry.com. There is a subscription fee.

Myth #1: You can find everything online.

If only this were true! You'll be able to find a lot of information online, but much of your family history sits in file cabinets and dusty shelves in library archives. Portions of the United States census are online. But if you want the whole census, you'll have to pay a subscription fee.

Myth #2: You can buy your family's coat of arms or family crest.

Many companies will offer to sell you your family's coat of arms. This is supposedly a design that your family has passed down through the ages. Don't believe it—there is no such thing. During the Middle Ages, a few individuals (not families) owned a coat of arms. They were not passed down, and they were not connected to surnames.

Above: Queen Elizabeth II's coat of arms is seen on many things in Great Britain today.

However, only a few individuals (not families) ever owned a family crest.

George Washington

King George III

Pocahontas

Above: Many people are descended from famous people, but not George Washington, who had no children.

Myth #3: Your family's name was changed at Ellis Island.

This is a common belief, but it is unlikely. The myth usually goes something like: "The clerks at Ellis Island couldn't understand (insert a language), so they just changed the name to something easy, like Stone, or Wolf." The truth is, when your family's first immigrants came to America, the immigration clerks were careful. Many spoke a variety of languages. If an immigrant's name got changed, it's more likely that the family, not the immigration clerks, Americanized their name so that they would fit in better in their new country.

Myth #4: You are descended from George Washington.

Or King George. Or Pocahontas. Everyone would like to be descended from someone famous. And, the truth is, many people *are* descended from someone famous. The rich and famous were able to keep better birth and death records than poor people. So, it's easier to trace the lineage of people who were wealthy. Some people are indeed able to trace their lineage back to someone famous. However, remember that the rich and famous often had very large families, who in turn had large families, and so on. Further, don't assume that just because your last name is Washington that you are descended from George Washington. Even when a surname is uncommon, you can't assume that you are related. (By the way, George Washington had no biological children. His wife, Martha, had two children from a previous marriage).

Above: Clerks at Ellis Island were careful to record immigrants' names. However, many new arrivals chose to Americanize their names to fit in better in their new country.

Getting Started

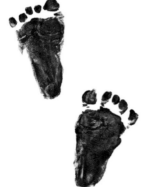

Start creating a family tree. The best place to begin is with what you know best: yourself. Put yourself on the page. Under your name, you can add your birthdate. Are you sure you were born on the day you usually celebrate as your birthday? Do you have a birth certificate to prove it?

Then, add your parents' names. Remember to use your mother's maiden name. If you know the years they were born, you can add those dates if you wish.

Then, add your grandparents' names and dates, if you know them. If you don't know the names, write "unknown."

Facing Page: A sample family tree with notations. *Right:* It's a good idea to get copies of your own and your family members' birth certificates to confirm the dates of birth.

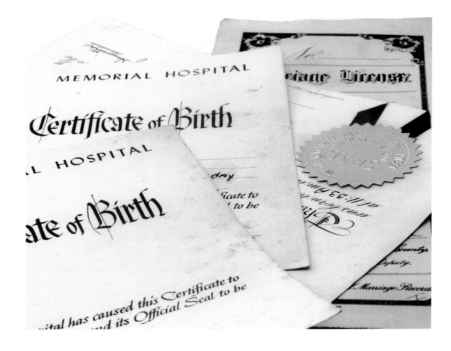

Family Tree
(with notations)

Albert Frederick
9/10/1952 –

Dad says Albert Frederick was born in 1952. There isn't a birth certificate because he was born in Germany.

Anthony Frederick
6/1/1979 –

Dad gave me a photocopy of his birth certificate and his marriage certificate.

Wanda Unknown
7/1/1954 – 12/30/1980

Dad never knew his mom and doesn't know her maiden name, but thinks she was born in Germany in 1954.

Kim Frederick
3/31/2000 –

Mom says my birth certificate is in the safe deposit box at the bank.

Craig Moore
2/18/1960 –

Mom is sure her dad was born in 1960 in New York City.

Susan Moore
1/14/1981 –

Mom says she was born in New York City. She says her birth certificate is in a box in the attic.

Clarice Franklin
5/16/1961 –

Grandma says she was born in 1961 in Rochester, New York.

Illustration 2

Craig Moore &
Clarice Franklin

Albert Frederick &
Wanda Unknown

Anthony Frederick &
Susan Moore

Above: You might want to make a file folder for each married couple in your family. Important documents, such as copies of birth and marriage certificates, can be placed inside each folder.

Talk to your parents, and find out if they can fill in any information. Remember to write down the source of the information, as in the example. Write down what your parents say, such as dates and cities of birth, but keep in mind that later you'll need to prove it with primary documents. Set aside a special place for the material you collect, such as copies of birth certificates. You might want to make a file folder for each married couple in your family.

Then, with your parents' permission, rummage through old boxes and file cabinets. Look for birth certificates, marriage certificates, and death certificates. Look for military records and passports. Look for newspaper clippings, or anything that might tell you information about your family's history.

Sometimes people keep family information in a special book, such as a family Bible. Perhaps someone in your family has already done some work on the family's history. If so, they will be a great source of information.

Above: Families sometimes recorded births, marriages, deaths, and other information in their Bible. It is a good source to use in researching your family tree.

What's Next?

Family history can be a lifelong hobby. You could spend the rest of your life filling in names, collecting documents, and jotting down family stories. Learning about the people who helped to make you what you are can be an exciting pastime.

The next step is perhaps to interview your grandparents. They might be a terrific source of information about your family's history. Contacting cousins can also add a lot of information about your common ancestors.

Collecting primary documents is an important part of family genealogical work. Collecting birth records, immigration and real estate records, death records, and other kinds of documents will help reconstruct the lives of your family.

It's also helpful to learn about the history at the time when your ancestors lived. What was it like to live without computers or the Internet? What kind of jobs did your ancestors have? What was going on in the world while they were living?

There are many exciting discoveries to be made in your family history. Enjoy the research!

Below: A portrait of a New York City fireman in July 1908. It's helpful to learn what kinds of jobs your ancestors had, as well as what was going on in the world when they were living.

Above: Interviewing your grandparents can be a terrific source of information about your family. Be sure to write down family stories, as well as who told them to you.

Glossary

ANCESTORS

The people from whom you are directly descended. Usually this refers to people in generations prior to your grandparents.

COLLATERAL FAMILY TREE

A record of family members that includes brothers and sisters and cousins, not just direct ancestors.

FAMILY LORE

Information that is passed down by word of mouth. Family lore can be helpful information, but it is often incorrect.

FAMILY TREE

A record of family members that includes those who are direct ancestors.

MATERNAL

Having to do with the mother's side of the family. Your maternal grandmother is your mother's mother.

MIDDLE AGES

In European history, the Middle Ages were a period defined by historians as roughly between 476 AD and 1450 AD.

PATERNAL

Having to do with the father's side of the family. Your paternal grandmother is your father's mother.

PEDIGREE CHART

A list of a person's ancestors as far back as is known.

PRIMARY SOURCE

A primary document is something created by an eyewitness to an event, someone who was there when the event happened. It can be an official document, like a birth certificate, or it can simply be a journal or letter written by an eyewitness. The sooner the document is created after the event, the better.

SURNAME

A person's last name.

Index